Simple Prayers for Everyday Life Situations

By
Michelle Jenkins

I0176756

Simple Prayers for Everyday Life Situations

Copyright 2017 by Michelle D. Jenkins

Published by Montsho Publishers

Available in Ebook and Paperback

Paperback ISBN 978-0-9679795-3-3

Scriptures based on NIV Bible

Dedication

To my son Christian, better known as my little surprise from GOD at forty.

Introduction

Everybody knows what praying is right? Well if you don't the simple definition is the act of talking to God. It's one of the greatest tools you can have and we all have this tool but we don't all use it. There are many reasons why people may not use it, but some feel they don't know how to use it. I'm one that used to feel that way. My reason was that I felt I wasn't doing it right. Well my belief now is that you can't actually do it wrong but there are some basic requirements.

1. Be comfortable and confident when you talk to God. God is like your BFF and you can talk to him about anything and he is listening plus he

loves you unconditionally. **(Proverbs 15:29)**

2. Be thankful in your prayer. Many people only talk to God when they need something. Your conversations with God should be all the time and not only when in need. Remember this is your friend, so laugh together and cry together. He is always there so be thankful for what he has done and for what he will do. **(John 3:16)**

3. Have faith in what you ask of him. This is where most people fall short. It's hard for some people to believe that God CAN and WILL provide. I say if you don't believe in what you ask, then why should he? It doesn't take much faith, as per **(Matthew 17:20)**, the faith of a grain of mustard seed can move mountains. So ask of God, believe in what you ask of God

and you shall receive from God. **(Matthew 21:22)**

So now that you know the basic requirements, you can feel more confident as you begin to talk to God. This should be something you do whenever you feel the urge. It can be in the car, at work or at night before you go to bed. There is no specific time or place you have to do it, be like Nike…Just Do It!

Then there are those that are already comfortable talking to God but don't feel comfortable praying in front of people. So when you're at Thanksgiving or Christmas dinner and they want somebody to pray. It's of course the same person that prays all the time like your Aunt Bessie or your uncle that's the self-proclaimed minister. Well this book will not only teach you how to pray but will also give you prayers you can use for various situations or occasions!

Once you learn and get comfortable with these prayers, you will be able to step up to the plate if called upon. Blessing the family meal, praying for a friend in need or giving thanks for the time spent with others. You will also learn how to create your own prayers. You will see after reviewing these prayers, there is no special formula to create a prayer. It's all about saying what's in your heart and letting God guide your tongue. You will see the words will start flowing faster than you think.

Well good luck in your quest to get closer to God. I have faith in you and know that God does too. All you have to do is take the first step and your path will be revealed, one step at a time.

Table of Contents

The Lord's Prayer

Our Father, which art in heaven

Hallowed be thy Name

Thy Kingdom come

Thy will be done in earth

As it is in heaven

Give us this day our daily bread

And forgive us our trespasses

As we forgive them that trespass against us

And lead us not into temptation

But deliver us from evil

For thine is the kingdom

The power, and the glory,

For ever and ever

Amen

(Matthew 6:9-13)

A Psalm of David

The Lord is my shepherd; I shall not want.

He makes me to lie down in green pastures;

He leads me beside the still waters.

He restores my soul;

He leads me in the paths of righteousness

for His name's sake.

Yea, though I walk through the valley of the

shadow of death, I will fear no evil; for You

are with me; Your rod and Your staff, they

comfort me You prepare a table before me in

the presence of my enemies; You anoint my

head with oil; My cup runs over.

Surely goodness and mercy shall follow me all

the days of my life; and I will dwell in the

house of the Lord forever.

(Psalms 23:1-6)

The Breakdown of Psalm 23

The Lord is my shepherd – **That's Relationship!**

I shall not want – **That's Supply!**

He makes me to lie down in green pastures – **That's Rest!**

He leads me beside the still waters – **That's Refreshment!**

He restores my soul – **That's Healing!**

He leads me in the paths of righteousness – **That's Guidance!**

For His name's sake – **That's Purpose!**

Yea, though I walk through the valley of the shadow of death – **That's Testing!**

I will fear no evil – **That's Protection!**

For You are with me – **That's Faithfulness!**

Your rod and Your staff, they comfort me —
That's Discipline!

You prepare a table before me in the presence
of my enemies — **That's Hope!**

You anoint my head with oil — **That's
Consecration!**

My cup runs over — **That's Abundance!**

Surely goodness and mercy shall follow me all
the days of my life — **That's Blessing!**

And I will dwell in the house of the Lord —
That's Security!

Forever — **That's Eternity!**

Prayers for Children

Nighttime

I hear no voice, I feel no touch, I see no glory
bright but yet I know that God is near in
darkness as in light. God watches ever by my
side, and hears my whispered prayer. A God
of love for a little child, both night and day
does care.

Amen

Now I lay me down to sleep.

I pray the Lord my soul to keep.

May angels watch me through the night,

and wake me with the morning light.

God bless our family and friends.

Amen

Angels bless and angels keep.

Angels guard me while I sleep.

Bless my heart and bless my home.

Bless my spirit as I roam.

Guide and guard me through the night

and wake me with the mornings light.

Amen

Matthew, Mark, Luke and John, bless the bed that I lie on. Before I lay me down to sleep, I pray the Lord my soul to keep. Four corners to my bed, four angels round my bed. One at my head, one at my feet and two to guard me while I sleep.

Amen

In peace I will lie down and sleep, for you alone, LORD, make me dwell in safety.

(Psalms 4:8)

Prayers for Children

Morning

Now before I run to play,

let me not forget to pray.

To God who kept me through the night and

waked me with the morning light. Help me

Lord to love thee more than I ever loved

before. In my work and in my play please be

with me throughout the day.

Amen

For this new morning with the light.

For the rest and shelter during the night.

For health and food, for love and friends.

For everything your goodness sends.

We thank you now and till the end.

Amen

Jesus help my feet to go, in the way that you
will show. Jesus help my hands to do, all
things loving, kind and true. Jesus guard me
through this day, in all I do and all I say.

Amen

Prayers for Children

Mealtime

Thank you for the world so sweet.

Thank you for the food we eat.

Thank you for the birds that sing.

Thank you God for everything.

Amen

Bless this food before us.

Bless the family and friends beside us.

Bless the love between us.

Thank you God for watching over us.

Amen

God our Father, Lord and Savior.

Thank you for your love and favor.

Bless this food and drink we pray

And all who shares with us today.

Amen

Lord thank you for the flowers and thank you
for the trees. Thank you for my friends and
all the fun they bring. Thank you for the
food I eat and thank you for my drink but
most of all I thank you God for the way that
you love me.

Amen

Reminder: Mealtime is family time. Spend as
much time enjoying the meal as it took to
prepare it.

Prayers for Children

Protection

Angel of God, my Guardian dear, to whom

God's love commits me here; ever this day, be

at my side, to light and guard,

to rule and guide.

Amen

Prayers for Children

Family & Friends

Father in heaven, hear my prayer. Keep me in
your loving care. Be my guide in all I do and
please bless those that love me too.

Amen

Our family is a circle of strength, founded on
faith, joined in love and kept by God.

Prayers for Today

Father thank you for filling me with your Holy Spirit. I ask you for guidance as I start my day and throughout. Direct my footsteps by your promise and do not let any kind of iniquity rule over me. I have no fear as I know you are with me and I can do all things through you. I surrender all to you in Jesus name we pray.

Amen

God thank you for your power working in
me. Thank you for equipping me and calling
me according to your purpose. Give me your
strength and peace today. I will keep my
mind stayed on you.

Amen

✝

Father I humbly come to you today giving
you all that I am. Mold me and shape me in
your image. Remove all in my life that is not
pleasing to you. I am your child, show me
your way.

Amen

God I thank you for the gift of another day.
My heart is filled with joy and I am thankful
for all that you have done and will do in my
life. I know I am nothing without you but
with you I am everything. I know you have
created me for a special purpose and you have
a plan for my life. I come to you each day
through prayer to ensure the choices I make
are in your best interest and in accordance to
your will. When my days on this earth are
done, I want to have used all the gifts you
have given me to bless others.

Amen

God I pray today that I show the world the person you have created. I ask nothing of you but thank you for everything. I worship you, I praise you and I place my life in your hands. No matter what comes my way, I know that you will light and guide my way.

Amen

This is the day the Lord has made. Let us rejoice and be glad in it. (Psalms 118:24)

Prayers for Forgiveness

Lord please forgive me for harboring anger and resentment. Give me the ability to forgive those that have hurt me. Help me guard my heart as emotions take over and try to keep my thoughts in the past where old wounds remain.

I know that you gave the ultimate sacrifice when you died for our sins. I do not take this lightly and I thank you for your gift. Lord please teach me to continuously appreciate all that I have and the others around me.

I know that not everybody in my life is on
my side but I know that you are and that is
more than enough and my cup runneth over
with your mercy and grace. I leave it in your
hands and trust in your guidance.

Dear Lord I am continually thankful for how
you continue to forgive me for all I have
done. You know I am not perfect but I strive
each day to do better.

Amen

Prayers for Love

Love is Patient, Love is Kind. It does not envy, It does not boast, It is not self-seeking. It is not easily angered. It keeps no records of wrongs. Love does not delight in evil but rejoices with the truth. It always protects, always trusts, always hopes, and always perseveres.

Amen

(I Corinthians 13:4-7)

God please guide me as I seek the person that
you have made for me. I know that I am not
perfect but I know there is a person that is
perfect for me. Open my heart and show me
how to be worthy of that love and only
choose a person that is worthy of me.
Let not the material things of this world blind
me as I seek because I know they can and will
fade but a love built on a solid foundation of
God will be tested but can be everlasting.

God prepare us both as we move through the stages of our relationship. Let us not forget what brought us together and to keep us moving closer to you.

True love doesn't have a happy ending, because true love never ends.
Real love doesn't care about body type, model looks, or wallet size.
It only cares about what's inside

Prayers for Healing

Heavenly Father we pray that you will lay your healing hands upon all those who are sick. We beg you to have compassion on all those who are suffering so that they may be delivered from their circumstances. In Jesus name we pray.

Amen

I pray that you be wrapped up in God's love, found deep in his everlasting wings, carried and kept safe and cherished. May the healing power of Christ breathe across your being right now and remove all that is ailing you. I know that God will touch you with his healing hand and give you the comfort and peace you need to get through.

Amen

Lord Jesus please heal me. Heal in me whatever you see needs healing. Heal me of whatever might separate me from you. Heal

my memory, my heart, my emotions, my

spirit, my body, and my soul. Lay your hands

gently upon me and heal me through your

love for me.

Amen

You will begin to heal only when you let go

of past hurts, forgive those who have wronged

you and learn to forgive yourself for your

mistakes.

Scriptures

ANGER:

Ephesians 4:26-27

"In your anger do not sin"; Do not let the sun go down while you are still angry, and do not give the devil a foothold.

Proverbs 29:11

Fools give vent to their rage, but the wise bring calm in the end.

Proverbs 29:22

An angry man stirs up dissension, and a hot-tempered one commits many sins.

James 1:19-20

My dear brothers, take note of this: Everyone should be quick to listen, slow to speak and slow to become angry, for man's anger does not bring about the righteous life that God desires.

Psalms 37:8-9

Refrain from anger and turn from wrath; do not fret – it leads only to evil. For those that are evil will be destroyed, but those who hope in the Lord will inherit the land.

Ecclesiastes 7:9

Do not be quickly provoked in your spirit, for anger resides in the lap of fools.

Psalms 145:8

The Lord is gracious and compassionate, slow to anger and rich in love.

Romans 12:19-21

Do not take revenge, my friends, but leave room for God's wrath, for it is written: "It is mine to avenge; I will repay," says the Lord. On the contrary: "If your enemy is hungry, feed him; if he is thirsty, give him something to drink. In doing this, you will heap burning coals

on his head." Do not be overcome by
evil, but overcome evil with good.

Ephesians 4:31-32

Get rid of all bitterness, rage and anger,
brawling and slander, along with every
form of malice. Be kind and
compassionate to one another,
forgiving each other, just in Christ God
forgave you.

BAPTISM:

Mark 1:9-11

And it came to pass in those days, that Jesus came from Nazareth of Galilee, and was baptized of John in Jordan. And straightway coming up out of the water, he saw the heavens opened, and the Spirit like a dove descending upon him: And there came a voice from heaven, *saying*, "Thou art my beloved Son, in whom I am well pleased."

Mark 16:16

He that believeth and is baptized shall be saved; but he that believeth not shall be damned.

Acts 22:16

And now what are you waiting for? Get up, be baptized and wash your sins away, calling on his name.

I Corinthians 12:13

"For by one Spirit are we all baptized into one body, whether we be Jews or Gentiles, whether we be bond or free; and have been all made to drink into one Spirit."

Romans 6:3-4

"Do you not know that all of us who have been baptized into Christ Jesus were baptized into his death? We were buried therefore with him by baptism into death, in order that, just as Christ was raised from the dead by the glory of the Father, we too might walk in newness of life."

CHILDREN:

Proverbs 22:6

Train up a child in the way he should go; even when he is old he will not depart from it.

Isaiah 54:13

All your children shall be taught by the Lord, and great shall be the peace of your children.

Proverbs 13:24

Whoever spares the rod hates his son, but he who loves him is diligent to discipline him.

Psalms 127:3-5

Behold, children are a heritage from the Lord, the fruit of the womb a reward. Like arrows in the hand of a warrior are the children of one's youth. Blessed is the man who fills his quiver with them! He shall not be put to shame when he speaks with his enemies in the gate.

James 1:17

Every good gift and every perfect gift is from above, coming down from the Father of lights with whom there is no variation or shadow due to change.

Proverbs 29:15

The rod and reproof give wisdom, but a child left to himself brings shame to his mother.

Psalms 139:13-16

For you formed my inward parts; you knitted me together in my mother's womb. I praise you, for I am fearfully and wonderfully made.Wonderful are your works; my soul knows it very well. My frame was not hidden from you,when I was being made in secret, intricately woven in the depths of the earth. Your eyes saw my unformed substance; in your book were written, every one of them, the days that were formed for me, when as yet there was none of them.

John 16:21

When a woman is giving birth, she has sorrow because her hour has come, but when she has delivered the baby, she no longer remembers the anguish, for joy that a human being has been born into the world.

Ephesians 6:4

Fathers, do not provoke your children to anger, but bring them up in the discipline and instruction of the Lord.

CHRISTMAS:

Isaiah 7:14

Therefore the Lord himself will give you a sign: The virgin will conceive and give birth to a son, and will call him Immanuel.

John 1:14

The Word became flesh and made his dwelling among us. We have seen his glory, the glory of the one and only Son, who came from the Father, full of grace and truth.

Galatians 4:4-5

But when the set time had fully come, God sent his Son, born of a woman, born under the law. To redeem those under the law, that we might receive adoption to sonship.

Romans 6:23

For the wages of sin is death, but the gift of God is eternal life in Christ Jesus our Lord.

John 3:16

For God so loved the world that he gave his one and only Son, that whoever believes in him shall not perish have eternal life.

1 John 5:11

And this is the testimony: God has given us eternal life, and this life is in his son.

Luke 2:14

"Glory to God in the highest heaven, and on earth peace to those on whom his favor rests."

COMFORT:

Psalms 138:7

Though I walk in the midst of trouble, you preserve my life, you stretch out your hand against the anger of my foes, with your right hand you save me.

Psalms 23:4

Even though I walk through the darkest valley, I will fear no evil, for you are with me; your rod and your staff, they comfort me.

John 14:27

Peace I leave with you; my peace I give you. I do not give to you as the world gives. Do not let your hearts be troubled and do not be afraid.

Matthew 11:28

"Come to me, all you who are weary and burdened, and I will give you rest."

Joshua 1:9

Have I not commanded you? Be strong and courageous. Do not be afraid; do not be discouraged, for the Lord your God will be with you wherever you go.

Psalms 37:24

Though he stumble, he will not fall, for the Lord upholds him with his hand.

COURAGE:

Psalms 37:3

Trust in the Lord and do good; dwell in the land and enjoy safe pasture.

2 Kings 6:16

"Don't be afraid," the prophet answered. "Those who are with us are more than those who are with them."

1 Chronicles 28:20

David also said to Solomon his son, "Be strong and courageous, and do the work. Do not be afraid or discouraged, for the Lord God, my God, is with you. He will not fail you or forsake you until all the work for the service of the temple of the Lord is finished.

Deuteronomy 31:6-8

Be strong and courageous. Do not be
afraid or terrified because of them, for
the Lord your God goes with you; he
will never leave you nor forsake you."
Then Moses summoned Joshua and said
to him in the presence of all Israel, "Be
strong and courageous, for you must
go with this people into the land that
the Lord swore to their ancestors to give
them, and you must divide it among
them as their inheritance. The Lord
himself goes before you and will be with
you; he will never leave you nor forsake
you. Do not be afraid; do not be
discouraged.

John 14:27

Peace I leave with you; my peace I give
you. I do not give to you as the world

gives. Do not let your hearts be troubled and do not be afraid.

Ephesians 6:10

Finally, be strong in the Lord and in his mighty power.

Psalms 27:1

The Lord is my light and my salvation- whom shall I fear? The Lord is the stronghold of my life- of whom shall I be afraid.

Philippians 4:12-13

I know what it is to be in need, and I know what it is to have plenty. I have learned the secret of being content in any and every situation, whether well fed or hungry, whether living in plenty or in want. I can do everything through him who gives me strength.

DEATH:

Luke 23:46

Jesus called out with a loud voice,
"Faather into your hands I commit my
spirit." When he had said this, he
breathed his last."

John 8:51

I tell you the truth, if a man keeps my
word, he will never see death."

Revelation:

Then I heard a voice from heaven say,
"Write this: Blessed are the dead who die
in the Lord from now on." "Yes," says
the Spirit, "they will rest from their
labor, for their deeds will follow them."

Psalms 48:14

For this God is our God for ever and
ever; he will be our guide even to the
end.

John 11:25-26

Jesus said to her, "I am the resurrection and the life. The one who believes in me will live, even though the die; and whoever lives by believing in me will never die. Do you believe this?"

Psalms 23:4

Even though I walk through the valley of the shadow of death, I will fear no evil for you are with me, your rod and your staff, they comfort me.

Hebrews 2:14-15

Since the children have flesh and blood, he too shared in their humanity so that by his death he might break the power of him who holds the power of death - that is, the devil - and free those who all their lives were held in slavery by their fear of death.

EASTER:

Mark 8:31

He then began to teach them that the Son of Man must suffer many things and be rejected by the elders, the chief priests and the teachers of the law, and that he must be killed and after three days rise again.

Mark 15:29-31

Those who passed by hurled insults at him, shaking their heads and saying, "So! You who are going to destroy the temple and build it in three days, come down from the cross and save yourself!" In the same way the chief priests and the teachers of the law mocked him among themselves. "He saved others," they said, "but he can't save himself!

John 19:5-6

When Jesus came out wearing the crown of thorns and the purple robe, Pilate said to them, "Here is the man! As soon as the chief priests and their officials saw him, they shouted, "Crucify! Crucify!" But Pilate answered, "You take him and crucify him. As for me, I find no basis for a charge against him."

Mark 15:46-47

So Joseph bought some linen cloth, took down the body, wrapped it in the linen, and placed it in a tomb cut out of rock. Then he rolled a stone against the entrance of the tomb. Mary Magdalene and Mary the mother of Joseph saw where he was laid.

Acts 3:15

You killed the author of life, but God raised him from the dead. We are witnesses of this.

Luke 24:6-7

He is not here; he has risen! Remember how he told you, while he was still with you in Galilee: 'The Son of Man must be delivered over to the hands of sinners, be crucified and on the third day be raised again.' "

Matthew 20:17-19

Now Jesus was going up to Jerusalem. On the way, he took the Twelve aside and said to them, "We are going up to Jerusalem, and the Son of Man will be delivered over to the chief priests and the teachers of the law. They will condemn him to death and will hand

him over to the Gentiles to be mocked
and flogged and crucified. On the third
day he will be raised to life!"

FAITH:

1 John 5:13

I write these things to you who believe in the name of the Son of God so that you may know that you have eternal life.

Galatians 2:20

I have been crucified with Christ and I no longer live, but Christ lives in me. The life I now live in the body, I live by faith in the Son of God, who loved me and game himself for me.

Romans 10:9

If you declare with your mouth, "Jesus is Lord," and believe in your heart that God raised him from the dead, you will be saved.

Mark 11:24

Therefore I tell you, whatever you ask for in prayer, believe that you have received it, and it will be yours.

John 3:36

Whoever believes in the Son has eternal life, but whoever rejects the Son will not see life, for God's wrath remains on them

Romans 1:17

For in the gospel the righteousness of God is revealed- a righteousness that is by faith from first to last, just as it is written: The righteous will live by faith."

John 3:16

For God so loved the world that he gave his one and only Son, that whoever believes in him shall not perish but have eternal life.

FAITHFULNESS:

2 Peter 3:9

The Lord is not slow in keeping his promise, as some understand slowness. He is patient with, not wanting anyone to perish, but everyone to come to repentance.

1 Samuel 15:29

"He who is the Glory of Israel does not lie or change his mind; for he is not a man, that he should change his mind."

2 Timothy 2:13

If we are faithless, he will remain faithful, for he cannot disown himself.

Isaiah 54:10

"Though the mountains be shaken and the hills be removed, yet my unfailing love for you will not be shaken nor my covenant of peace be removed," says the Lord, who has compassion on you.

Hebrew 10:23

Let us hold fast the confession of our hope without wavering, for he who promised is faithful.

1 Corinthians 10:13

No temptation has overtaken you that is not common to man. God is faithful, and he will not let you be tempted beyond your ability, but with the temptation he will also provide the way of escape, that you may be able to endure it.

Lamentations 3:22-23

Because of the LORD's great love we are not consumed, for his compassions never fail. They are new every morning; great is your faithfulness.

Psalms 36:5

Your steadfast love, O Lord, extends to
the heavens, your faithfulness to the
clouds.

FEAR:

Isaiah 41:13

For I am the Lord, your God, who takes hold of your right hand and says to you, do not dear; I will help you.

Proverbs 1:33

"But whoever listens to me will live in safety and be at ease, without fear of harm.

Psalms 27:1

The Lord is my light and my salvation – whom shall I fear? The Lord is the stronghold of my life – of whom shall I be afraid?

Psalms 118:6

The Lord is with me; I will not be afraid. What can mere mortals do to me?

Psalms 27:1-3

The LORD is my light and my salvation — whom shall I fear? The LORD is the stronghold of my life— of whom shall I be afraid? When the wicked advance against me to devour me, it is my enemies and my foes who will stumble and fall. Though an army besiege me, my heart will not fear; though war break out against me, even then I will be confident.

Romans 8:37-39

No, in all these things we are more than conquerors through him who loved us. For I am convinced that neither death nor life, neither angels nor demons, neither the present nor the future, nor any powers, neither height nor depth, nor anything else in all creation, will be able to separate us from the love of God that is in Christ Jesus our Lord.

FORGIVENESS:

Mark 11:25

And when you stand praying, if you hold anything against anyone, forgive him, so that your Father in heaven may forgive you your sins.

Matthew 6:14-15

For if you forgive men when they sin against you, your heavenly Father will also forgive you. But if you do not forgive others their sins, your Father will not forgive your sins.

Ephesians 4:31-32

Get rid of all bitterness, rage and anger, brawling and slander, along with every form of malice. Be kind and compassionate to one another, forgiving each other, just as in Christ God forgave you.

Luke 6:35-38

But love your enemies, do good to them, and lend to them without expecting to get anything back. Then your reward will be great, and you will be children of the Most High, because he is kind to the ungrateful and wicked. Be merciful, just as your Father is merciful. "Do not judge, and you will not be judged. Do not condemn, and you will not be condemned. Forgive, and you will be forgiven. Give, and it will be given to you. A good measure, pressed down, shaken together and running over, will be poured into your lap. For with the measure you use, it will be measured to you."

Daniel 9:9

The Lord our God is merciful and forgiving, even though we have rebelled against him.

GOSSIP:

Leviticus 19:16

" 'Do not go about spreading slander among your people. " 'Do not do anything that endangers your neighbor's life. I am the LORD.' "

Proverbs 10:18

Whoever conceals hatred with lying lips and spreads slander is a fool.

Psalms 34:13

Keep your tongue from evil and your lips from telling lies.

Proverbs 18:6-7

The lips of fools bring them strife, and their mouths invite a beating. The mouths of fools are their undoing, and their lips are a snare to their very lives.

1 Timothy 5:13-14

Besides, they get into the habit of being idle and going about from house to house. And not only do they become idlers, but also busybodies who talk nonsense, saying things they ought not to. So I counsel younger widows to marry, to have children, to manage their homes and to give the enemy no opportunity for slander.

Proverbs 26:20-22

Without wood a fire goes out; without a gossip a quarrel dies down. As charcoal to embers and as wood to fire, so is a quarrelsome person for kindling strife. The words of a gossip are like choice morsels, they go down to the inmost parts.

Psalm 141:3

Set a guard over my mouth, LORD,
keep watch over the door of my lips.

GUIDANCE:

Psalms 73:23-24

Yet I am always with you; you hold me by my right hand. You guide me with your counsel, and afterward you will take me into glory.

Isaiah 30:21

Whether you turn to the right or to the left, your ears will hear a voice behind you saying, "This is the way; walk in it."

1 Corinthians 12:28

And God has placed in the church first of all apostles, second prophets, third teachers, then miracles, then gifts of healing, of helping, of guidance, and of different kinds of tongues.

Psalms 32:8

I will instruct you and teach you in the way you should go; I will counsel you and watch over you.

Isaiah 42:16

I will lead the blind by ways they have not known, along unfamiliar paths I will guide them; I will turn the darkness into light before them and make the rough places smooth. These are the things I will do; I will not forsake them.

Psalms 37:23

The Lord delights in the way of the man whose steps he has made firm.

Proverbs 3:6

In all your ways acknowledge him, and he will make your paths straight.

Isaiah 28:26

His God instructs him and teaches him
the right way.

Psalms 48:14

For this God is our God for ever and
ever; he will be our guide even to the
end.

GUILT:

Isaiah 43:25

"I, even I, am he who blots out your transgressions, for my own sake, and remembers your sins no more."

1 John 1:7

But if we walk in the light, as he is in the light, we have fellowship with one another, and the blood of Jesus, his Son, purifies us from all sin.

Jeremiah 31:34

No longer will they teach their neighbor, or say to one another, 'Know the LORD,' because they will all know me, from the least of them to the greatest," declares the LORD." For I will forgive their wickedness and will remember their sins no more."

Psalms 103:12

As far as the east is from the west, so far has he removed our transgressions from us.

2 Chronicles 30:9

"If you return to the Lord, then your brothers and your children will be shown compassion by their captors and will come back to this land, for the Lord your God is gracious and compassionate. He will not turn his face from you if you return to him."

1 John 1:9

If we confess our sins, he is faithful and just and will forgive us our sins and purify us from all unrighteousness.

Hebrews 8:12

"For I will forgive their wickedness and will remember their sins no more.

HONESTY:

2 Timothy 2:15

Do your best to present yourself to God as one approved, a worker who does not need to be ashamed and who correctly handles the word of truth.

Colossians 3:9

Do not lie to each other, since you have taken off your old self with its practices

Leviticus 19:11

"'Do not steal. "'Do not lie. "'Do not deceive one another.

Psalms 37:21

The wicked borrow and do not repay, but the righteous give generously.

Proverbs 16:8

Better a little with righteousness than much gain with injustice.

1 John 3:18

Dear children, let us not love with words or speech but with actions and in truth.

Proverbs 21:3

To do what is right and just is more acceptable to the Lord than sacrifice.

Romans 13:7

Give to everyone what you owe them: If you owe taxes, pay taxes; if revenue, then revenue; if respect, then respect; if honor, then honor.

Psalms 37:7

Be still before the Lord and wait patiently for him; do not fret when people succeed in their ways, when they carry out their wicked schemes.

Matthew 5:8

Blessed are the pure in heart, for they will see God.

JEALOUSY:

James 3:16

For where you have envy and selfish ambition, there you find disorder and every evil practice.

Proverbs 3:11

Do not envy a violent man or choose any of his ways.

Luke 12:22-23

Then Jesus said to his disciples: "Therefore I tell you, do not worry about your life, what you will eat; or about your body, what you will wear. For life is more than food, and the body more than clothes.

Galatians 5:26

Let us not become conceited, provoking and envying each other.

Proverbs 24:1

Do not envy wicked men, do not desire their company.

Psalms 37:7

Be still before the Lord and wait patiently for him; do not fret when men succeed in their ways, when they carry out their wicked schemes.

Proverbs 23:17-18

Do not let your heart envy sinners, but always be zealous for the fear of the LORD. There is surely a future hope for you, and your hope will not be cut off.

Ecclesiastes 4:4

And I saw that all toil and all achievement spring from one person's envy of another. This too is meaningless, a chasing after the wind.

LAZINESS:

Proverbs 24:30-34

I went past the field of a sluggard, past the vineyard of someone who has no sense; thorns had come up everywhere, the ground was covered with weeds, and the stone wall was in ruins. I applied my heart to what I observed and learned a lesson from what I saw: A little sleep, a little slumber, a little folding of the hands to rest— and poverty will come on you like a thief and scarcity like an armed man.

Ephesians 4:28

He who has been stealing must steal no longer, but must work, doing something useful with his own hands, that he may have something to share with those in need.

Proverbs 12:11

He who works his land will have abundant food, but he who chases fantasies lacks judgment.

Ecclesiastes 5:18-19

This is what I have observed to be good: that it is appropriate for a person to eat, to drink and to find satisfaction in their toilsome labor under the sun during the few days of life God has given them— for this is their lot. Moreover, when God gives someone wealth and possessions, and the ability to enjoy them, to accept their lot and be happy in their toil—this is a gift of God.

2 Timothy 2:6

The hard-working farmer should be the first to receive a share of the crops.

LONELINESS:

Genesis 28:15

"I am with you and will watch over you wherever you go, and I will bring you back to this land. I will not leave you until I have done what I have promised you."

Psalms 40:17

Yet I am poor and needy; may the Lord think of me. You are my help and my deliverer; O my God, do not delay.

2 Corinthians 6:18

"I will be a Father to you, and you will be my sons and daughters, says the Lord Almighty."

Isaiah 58:9

Then you will call, and the Lord will answer; you will cry for help, and he will say: Here am I.

John 14:18

I will not leave you as orphans; I will come to you.

Colossians 2:10

And you have been given fullness in Christ, who is the head over every power and authority.

LOVE:

Romans 13:8

Let no debt remain outstanding, except the continuing debt to love one another, for whoever loves others has fulfilled the law.

1 John 4:20

Whoever claims to love God yet hates a brother or sister is a liar. For whoever does not love their brother and sister, whom they have seen, cannot love God, whom they have not seen.

1 Corinthians 13:4:5

Love is patient, love is kind. It does not envy, it does not boast, it is not proud. It does not dishonor others, it is not self-seeking, it is not easily angered, it keeps no record of wrongs.

Proverbs 3:3-4

Let love and faithfulness never leave you; bind them around your neck, write them on the tablet of your heart. Then you will win favor and a good name in the sight of God and man.

Psalms 103:8

The Lord is compassionate and gracious, slow to anger, abounding in love.

Song of Songs 8:6

Place me like a seal over your heart, like a seal on your arm; for love is as strong as death, its jealousy unyielding as the grave. It burns like blazing fire, like a mighty flame.

Galatians 5:14

For the entire law is fulfilled in keeping this one command: "Love your neighbor as yourself."

LUST:

James 4:1-4

What causes fights and quarrels among you? Don't they come from your desires that battle within you? You desire but do not have, so you kill. You covet but you cannot get what you want, so you quarrel and fight. You do not have because you do not ask God. When you ask, you do not receive, because you ask with wrong motives, that you may spend what you get on your pleasures. You adulterous people, don't you know that friendship with the world means enmity against God? Therefore, anyone who chooses to be a friend of the world becomes an enemy of God.

Proverbs 6:25-29

Do not lust in your heart after her beauty or let her captivate you with her eyes. For a prostitute can be had for a loaf of bread, but another man's wife preys on your very life. Can a man scoop fire into his lap without his clothes being burned? Can a man walk on hot coals without his feet being scorched? So is he who sleeps with another man's wife; no one who touches her will go unpunished.

James 1:13

When tempted, no one should say, "God is tempting me." For God cannot be tempted by evil, nor does he tempt anyone.

LYING:

Leviticus 19:12

" 'Do not sear falsely by my name and so profane the name of your God. I am the Lord.' "

Zachariah 8:17

"Do not plot evil against your neighbor, and do not love to swear falsely. I hate all this," declares the Lord.

Proverbs 19:5

A false witness will not go unpublished, and he who pours lies will not go free.

Colossians 3:9-10

Do not lie to each other, since you have taken off your old self with its practices and have put on the new self, which is being renewed in knowledge in the image of its Creator.

Proverbs 25:18

Like a club or a sword or a sharp arrow is the man who gives false testimony against his neighbor.

Exodus 23:1

"Do not spread false reports. Do not help a wicked man by being a malicious witness."

Proverbs 14:15

A truthful witness does not deceive, but a false witness pours out lies.

James 3:14

But if you harbor bitter envy and selfish ambition in your hearts, do not boast about it or deny the truth.

Proverbs 19:9

A false witness will not go unpunished and he who pours out lies will perish.

MARRIAGE:

Colossians 3:18-19

Wives, submit yourselves to your husbands, as is fitting in the Lord. Husbands, love your wives and do not be harsh with them.

Matthew 19:4-6

"Haven't you read," he replied, "that at the beginning the Creator 'made them male and female,' and said, 'For this reason a man will leave his father and mother and be united to his wife, and the two will become one flesh'? So they are no longer two, but one flesh. Therefore what God has joined together, let no one separate."

1 Corinthians 7:2

But since sexual immorality is occurring, each man should have sexual relations with his own wife, and each woman with her own husband.

Ephesians 5:25-26

Husbands, love your wives, just as Christ loved the church and gave himself up for her to make her holy, cleansing her by the washing with water through the word.

Genesis 2:22-24

Then the Lord God made a woman from the rib he had taken out of the man, and he brought her to the man. The man said, "This is now bone of my bones and flesh of my flesh; she shall be called 'woman,' for she was taken out of man." That is why a man leaves his father and mother and is united to his wife, and they become one flesh.

Deuteronomy 24:5

If a man has recently married, he must not be sent to war or have any other duty laid on him. For one year he is to be free to stay at home and bring happiness to the wife he has married.

MONEY:

Proverbs 23:4-5

Do not wear yourself out to get rich; do not trust your own cleverness. Cast but a glance at riches, and they are gone, for they will surely sprout wings and fly off to the sky like an eagle.

1 Timothy 6:17-19

Command those who are rich in this present world not to be arrogant nor to put their hope in wealth, which is so uncertain, but to put their hope in God, who richly provides us with everything for our enjoyment. Command them to do good, to be rich in good deeds, and to be generous and willing to share. In this way they will lay up treasure for themselves as a firm foundation for the coming age, so that they may take hold of the life that is life.

Deuteronomy 8:18

But remember the Lord your God, for it is he who gives you the ability to produce wealth, and so confirms his covenant, which he swore to your forefathers, as it is today.

James 2:5

Listen, my dear brothers: Has not God chosen those who are poor in the eyes of the world do be rich in faith and to inherit the kingdom he promised those who love him?

Psalm 37:16-17

Better the little that the righteous have than the wealth of many wicked; for the power of the wicked will be broken, but the Lord upholds the righteous.

Proverbs 28:22

A stingy man is eager to get rich and is unaware that poverty awaits him.

Matthew 25:21

His master replied, 'Well done, good and faithful servant! You have been faithful with a few things; I will put you in charge of many things. Come and share your master's happiness!'

Proverbs 11:28

Whoever trusts in his riches will fall, but the righteous will thrive like a green leaf.

Luke 12:15

Then he said to them, "Watch out! Be on your guard against all kinds of greed; life does not consist in an abundance of possessions."

Proverbs 22:1

A good name is more desirable than great riches; to be esteemed is better than silver or gold.

PATIENCE:

Galatians 6:9

Let us not become weary in doing good, for at the proper time we will reap a harvest if we do not give up.

Psalms 37:7

Be still before the Lord and wait patiently for him; do not fret when people succeed in their ways, when they carry out their wicked schemes.

James 5:7-8

Be patient, then, brothers and sisters, until the Lord's coming. See how the farmer waits for the land to yield its valuable crop, patiently waiting for the autumn and spring rains. 8 You too, be patient and stand firm, because the Lord's coming is near.

James 1:2-4

Consider it pure joy, my brothers and sisters, whenever you face trials of many kinds, because you know that the testing of your faith produces perseverance. Let perseverance finish its work so that you may be mature and complete, not lacking anything.

Hebrew 10:36

You need to persevere so that when you have done the will of God, you will receive what he has promised.

Galatians 6:9

Let us not become weary in doing good, for at the proper time we will reap a harvest if we do not give up.

Exodus 14:14

The Lord will fight for you; you need only to be still.

PRIDE:

1 John 2:16

For everything in the world—the lust of the flesh, the lust of the eyes, and the pride of life—comes not from the Father but from the world.

Proverbs 8:13

To fear the Lord is to hate evil; I hate pride and arrogance, evil behavior and perverse speech.

Luke 16:15

He said to them, "You are the ones who justify yourselves in the eyes of men, but God knows your hearts. What is highly valued among men is detestable in God's sight."

Proverbs 11:2

When pride comes, then comes disgrace, but with humility comes wisdom.

2 Corinthians 10:17-18

But, "Let the one who boasts boast in the Lord." For it is not the one who commends himself who is approved, but the one whom the Lord commends.

John 5:44

How can you believe if you accept praise from one another, you make no effort to obtain the praise that comes from the only God?

1 Samuel 16:7

But the Lord said to Samuel, "Do not consider his appearance or his height, for I have rejected him. The Lord does not look at the things people look at.

People look at the outward appearance,
but the Lord looks at the heart."

Proverbs 27:2

Let another praise you, and not your
own mouth; someone else, and not
your own lips.

PROTECTION:

Hebrews 13:6

So we say with confidence, "The Lord is my helper; I will not be afraid. What can mere mortals do to me?"

Exodus 14:14

The Lord will fight for you; you need only to be still.

Psalms 34:22

The Lord will rescue his servants; no one who takes refuge in him will be condemned.

Isaiah 54:17

"No weapon forged against you will prevail, and you will refute every tongue that accuses you. This is the heritage of the servants of the Lord, and this is their vindication from me," declares the Lord.

Deuteronomy 31:6

Be strong and courageous. Do not be afraid or terrified because of them, for the Lord your God goes with you; he will never leave you nor forsake you.

Ephesians 6:11

Put on the full armor of God, so that you can take your stand against the devil's schemes.

2 Timothy 4:18

The Lord will rescue me from every evil attack and will bring me safely to his heavenly kingdom. To him be glory for ever and ever. Amen.

2 Samuel 22:31

As for God, his way is perfect: The Lord's word is flawless; he shields all who take refuge in him.

REPENTANCE:

2 Peter 3:9

The Lord is not slow in keeping his promise, as some understand slowness. Instead he is patient with you, not wanting anyone to perish, but everyone to come to repentance.

Acts 2:38

Peter replied, "Repent and be baptized, every one of you, in the name of Jesus Christ for the forgiveness of your sins. And you will receive the gift of the Holy Spirit."

Revelation 3:19

Those whom I love I rebuke and discipline. So be earnest and repent.

Acts 17:30

In the past God overlooked such ignorance, but now he commands all people everywhere to repent.

Luke 15:7

I tell you that in the same way there will be more rejoicing in heaven over one sinner who repents than over ninety-nine righteous persons who do not need to repent.

Ezekiel 18:21

"But if a wicked person turns away from all the sins they have committed and keeps all my decrees and does what is just and right, that person will surely live; they will not die. 22 None of the offenses they have committed will be remembered against them. Because of the righteous things they have done, they will live.

Mark 1:15

"The time has come," he said. "The kingdom of God is near. Repent and believe the good news!"

SEXUAL SIN:

2 Corinthians 12:21

I am afraid that when I come again my God will humble me before you, and I will be grieved over many who have sinned earlier and not repented of the impurity, sexual sin and debauchery in which they have indulged.

Ephesians 5:1-3

Follow God's example, therefore, as dearly loved children and walk in the way of love, just as Christ loved us and gave himself up for us as a fragrant offering and sacrifice to God.   But among you there must not be even a hint of sexual immorality, or of any kind of impurity, or of greed, because these are improper for God's holy people.

Genesis 2:24

The acts of the flesh are obvious: sexual immorality, impurity and debauchery.

Hebrews 13:4

Marriage should be honored by all, and the marriage bed kept pure, for God will judge the adulterer and all the sexually immoral.

1 Corinthians 6:18

Flee from sexual immorality. All other sins a person commits are outside the body, but whoever sins sexually, sins against their own body.

Matthew 5:28

But I tell you that anyone who looks at a woman lustfully has already committed adultery with her in his heart.

SHAME:

2 Timothy 2:15

Do your best to present yourself to God as one approved, a workman who does not need to be ashamed and who correctly handles the word of truth.

1 Peter 4:16

However, if you suffer as a Christian, do not be ashamed, but praise God that you bear that name.

Romans 10:11

As the Scripture says, "Everyone who trusts in him will never be put to shame.

Luke 9:26

Whoever is ashamed of me and my words, the Son of Man will be ashamed of them when he comes in his glory and in the glory of the Father and of the holy angels.

SICKNESS:

Luke 4:40

At sunset, the people brought to Jesus all who had various kings of sickness, and laying his hands on each one, he healed them.

Jeremiah 17:14

Heal me, O Lord, and I will be healed; save me and I will be saved, for you are the one I praise.

Mattew 9:28-30

When he had gone indoors, the blind men came to him, and he asked them, "Do you believe that I am able to do this? "Yes, Lord," they replied. Then he touched their eyes and said," According to your faith will it be done to you"; and their sight was restored. Jesus warned them sternly, "See that no one knows about this."

James 5:14-16

Is any one of you sick? He should call the elders of the church to pray over him and anoint him with oil in the name of the Lord, And the prayer offered in faith will make the sick person well; the Lord will raise him up. If he has sinned, he will be forgiven. Therefore confess your sins to each other and pray for each other so that you may be healed.   The prayer of a righteous man is powerful and effective.

Exodus 15:26

He said, "If you listen carefully to the Lord your God and do what is right in his eyes, if you pay attention to his commands and keep all his decrees, I will not bring on you any of the diseases I brought on the Egyptians, for I am the Lord, who heals you."

SUCCESS:

Philippians 4:13

I can do all this through him who gives me strength.

Psalms 37:4

Take delight in the Lord, and he will give you the desires of your heart.

Proverbs 16:3

Commit to the Lord whatever you do, and he will establish your plans.

Matthew 16:26-27

What good will it be for someone to gain the whole world, yet forfeit their soul? Or what can anyone give in exchange for their soul? For the Son of Man is going to come in his Father's glory with his angels, and then he will reward each person according to what they have done.

Ecclesiastes 5:19

Moreover, when God gives any man wealth and possessions, and enables him to enjoy them, to accept his lot and be happy in his work – this is a gift of God.

Deuteronomy 28:11–13

The Lord will make you the head, not the tail. If you pay attention to the commands of the Lord your God that I give you this day and carefully follow them, you will always be at the top, never at the bottom.

Psalms 128:2

You will eat the fruit of your labor; blessings and prosperity will be yours.

Philippians 4:6

Do not be anxious about anything, but in every situation, by prayer and petition, with thanksgiving, present your requests to God.

THANKSGIVING:

1 Thessalonians 5:18

Give thanks in all circumstances, for this is God's will for you in Christ Jesus.

Isaiah 12:4

In that day you will say: "Give praise to the Lord, proclaim his name; make known among the nations what he has done, and proclaim that his name is exalted.

Psalms 106:1

Praise the Lord. Give thanks to the Lord, for he is good; his love endures forever.

1 Timothy 4:4-5

For everything God created is good, and nothing is to be rejected if it is received with thanksgiving, because it is consecrated by the word of God and prayer.

TRUST:

Psalms 9:10

Those who know your name trust in you, for you, Lord, have never forsaken those who seek you.

Proverbs 11:28

Those who trust in their riches will fall, but the righteous will thrive like a green leaf.

Daniel 6:23

The king was overjoyed and gave orders to lift Daniel out of the den. And when Daniel was lifted from the den, no wound was found on him, because he had trusted in his God.

Romans 15:13

May the God of hope fill you with all joy and peace as you trust in him, so that you may overflow with hope by the power of the Holy Spirit.

Proverbs 11:13

A gossip betrays a confidence, but a trustworthy person keeps a secret.

Revelation 21:5

He who was seated on the throne said, "I am making everything new!" Then he said, "Write this down, for these words are trustworthy and true."

Proverbs 3:5-6

Trust in the Lord with all your heart and lean not on your own understanding; in all your ways submit to him, and he will make your paths straight.

Psalms 84:11-12

For the Lord God is a sun and shieeld; the Lord bestows favor and honor; no good thing does he withhold from those whose walk is blameless. O Lord

Almighty, blessed is the man who trusts in you.

WISDOM:

James 1:5

If any of you lacks wisdom, you should ask God, who gives generously and to all without finding fault, and it will be given to you.

2 Corinthians 4:6

For God, who said, "let light shine out of darkness," made his light shine in our hearts to give us light of the knowledge of the glory of God in the face of Christ.

Job 12:12

Is not wisdom found among the aged? Does not long life bring understanding?

Psalms 32:8

I will instruct you and teach you in the way you should go; I will counsel you and watch over you.

Ecclesiastes 2:26

To the man that pleases him, God gives wisdom, knowledge and happiness but to the sinner he gives the task of gathering and storing up wealth to hand it over to the one who pleases God. This too is meaningless, a chasing after the wind.

Proverbs 1:7

The fear of the Lord is the beginning of knowledge, but fools despise wisdom and instruction.

1 Corinthians 1:25

For the foolishness of God is wiser than human wisdom, and the weakness of God is stronger than human strength.

Psalms 16:7

I will praise the Lord, who counsels me; even at night my heart instructs me.

One Last Thing

About The Author

Michelle is the author of several books of various genres from children's mystery books to self-help. She is a native of North Carolina and currently resides in South Carolina with her family.

Other Books by the Author:

The Case of the Skunked Out Bash

A mystery book for ages 7 – 12, about four 10 year old detectives: Jerome, Mega-Byte, Equation and Rock. Join them as they solve their first case of the summer in this Super Sleuth Mystery! (ISBN 978-0-9679795-1-9)

Slightly Twisted Words of Wisdom and Other Funny Sayings

A book of funny quotes and sayings to pick up when you need some inspiration, motivation, or just a good dose of laughter. Grouped in 16 categories from college to relationships, you will find just what you need. (ISBN 978-0-9679795-2-6)

All books available on Amazon!